Bury Me in the Sky

Sara Comito

Nixes Mate Books
Allston, Massachusetts

Copyright © 2020 Sara Comito

Book design by d'Entremont
Cover photograph by Mike Kiniry

All rights reserved. This book or any portion thereof may not be reproduced or used in any manner whatsoever without the express written permission of the publisher except for the use of brief quotations in a book review or scholarly journal.

ISBN 978-1-949279-24-5

Nixes Mate Books
POBox 1179
Allston, MA 02134
nixesmate.pub/books

For John

Contents

OUR POOR MAGIC
Sweet Formication … 1
All Drains Lead to the Sea … 2
Lost Mooring … 3
Buried … 4
A Charming Rub … 6
Time out of Place … 8
Historical Constraint … 9
Listing … 10
Florida Dreams of Peru … 12
Once Again at the Stove … 13

MAKE ME A TOMB OF FISHES
The Germ Suspended … 15
In Tidal Relief … 17
Iodine … 18
Spill … 20
The Smell of Honey … 22
Florida's New Space Program … 23
Permission to expand … 25
Vengeance … 26
Dry … 28
Not for Long … 29

ANY MIGRATION IS FORCED
7 Billion … 31

The Flea Market Sells our Sacred Origins from Under Us	32
If Blake Had Only Known	33
Religion at the City Pier	34
Night in the Tropics	35
The Skill in Gravity	37
Any Migration is Forced	39
Pieces of the Poet	40
7 Years for Us	42

WHAT CAN NEVER BE BURIED

A personal Stonehenge	45
Overdone	47
Microscopic	49
Sounds Like Leaving	50
Consider the Living	52
Blizzard, 2015	53
Bury Me in the Sky	54
Dedication	56

SARGASSO

Pristine Creature	58
Hepatic Portal Dreaming	60
Sargasso	61
Husk of a Whale	62
Texas Radio, 1971	63
Dark Island Landing	65
All There Is	67

Bury Me in the Sky

Our Poor Magic

Sweet Formication

the ants want to eat my honey

a little finger finesse
and they're eating it alright
like the mosquito in the amber

how many lifeforms in the way
an armageddon in a sheet washing
all our tries down the drain

and there hasn't been enough
trying

sheep laurel, orange blossom
oleander nectar of Min,
the bear squeezer it all came in

if there's poetry in this sacking,
it's that food meant for one queen has
at least gone to another

All Drains Lead to the Sea

The iris in its exigency strives only
to flower. These things are of a marshy sort
and a far way from any Africa.

How did I think I could serve? This soil
is bereft, with only mocking water
below, so catacombed in chalk.

There have been people lately diving to chart
the aquifer. The support staff shadows above
ground, beacon squealing as those below veer in
and out of range, bushwhacking through
swales, through supermarkets,
knocking on residences.

Would they know, from a slow contrary course,
of the intrepid demise and follow to the output
- *all drains lead to the sea* - after losing one on the mic?

Here is only silt. Precambria stress testing the botany.

Lost Mooring

Awake – point it north.
Account for any chocolate onboard.
What floats? Wreckage, promise,

same thing. A coral head disruption betrays
itself in moon betrayed again by some rumored
sun. Driftwood is no rumor but is better than a shell
mound which would be hard to explain in this much
moon.

It may also be what we need.
But back to my nautical authority: I've at least never hit
any mammals.

Buried

You can get a horse as soon
as you get a backhoe big
enough to bury it, Momma
told her. Likewise, she didn't
have the smarts to bother
with college.

Down the pier a sailor smoked
and mended his net. Feeling her
stare, he pegged her for
lonely, took her out to sea.
Momma didn't get a husband
til she had a big enough knife.
The net was big enough for this
new catch, but – Momma
will be missing me.

His face cracked with years
of salt like those sore, handknitted
knots. Swells made false islands
of horizon. Seven miles and you
lose the land, he says.

The distance she can't make
sense of. It folds itself into a wave
she could ride all the way back there
and bury everything. But she can't tell.
Is it big enough?

A Charming Rub

Even indoors where sunlight is at my
whim morning glories open
and close to show me the season of day.

Even without water would locks
show me the tides of rivers and their
100 miles and be but barn doors
for sheep, and sheep tons of gravity
in their warmth of comfort.

Surrender is a charming rub
and in a decade of stillness
we build our houses
in the shelter of the volcano.
We keep our fires in those houses,
our poor magic burning under the stew.
And in the whisper moment
between the devastation of contraction
a woman hears the mountain moan
and, ripping, heaves forth blood and child.

Even without a face of moon
the tides know a jealous mother
and a borrowing planet's tenuous ministry.

Even in its mating does a wolf
know the taste of a foal –
newly standing, newly felled.

Time out of Place

The sky is disabused of sparrows.
It is bereft, for it does not grieve. At
the gravesite do stand the bereaved.
It is not something they've done to
themselves. Doves burn up in the
sunset. A few men let fall embers
from shadows of downturned fedoras.

There is no place for time after it's
eaten off all the plates. We shoo the
cats for lesser offense. The cold will
have us off now, the happy cold,
granting us excuse, mumbled to stave
the sincere exercises we've practiced
but are loathe to enlist. Keep them
under your coat. Of chattered niceties
we are happily bereft, and no one
has chosen to host. Turn your fur-lined
backs on this garden of ago. The chill,

sickly twin of cold, looks always
for someone who lingers too long.

Historical Constraint

Had to take a ride past the old house
where we had that sex we had that fight.
Moved the bed to the living room, moved
the boy to the back. That mango tree. Too
high to ever pick and the fruit spoils in a
plague of flies. The old lines make no sense.
French doors opening to the reggaeton.

Listing

Goals for tonight:
    fly from rocky cliffs
    swim with otters
    simplify the tax code
    engage in a trite oneuppance
    with a drunk cummings

sleep it off
    and dream

To do:
    plumb the more modern lines
    do something Zen
    use Zen as an adverb
    catch my neighbor's eye
    as he does laundry
    hang mine in surrender

hear it flap in the breeze. It's so nice
to be under something else's power
and let it be like sailing,
which I've never done
    and dream

does it rock so —
>   or so?

Sew a blanket with sleeves
make a million bucks
shear a sheep — shear anything!
And sell the wool for a trout.
Make breakfast.
Done.

Florida Dreams of Peru

Kiln dried mummies, landscape of once were alpacas.
Now all the wool is farmed in Alva, whose town museum
opens one day a week. Also: it's very warm here.

The llamas they use to guard the sheep. More
vicious than dogs, they say, and better insinuators
for their unwolvenness. They grind rather than
tear. The Calusa would be confounded!

Well how appropriate would it be to have camels
running around under the orange trees, humps
bumping all that Spanish fruit? Better to
leave blankets on the desertification,

those Nazca scars of ash; we have our epiphytic moss, but
really need less softening. There's a picture of an eagle
soaring over Peru. Wingspan of my palm.

Everything concentric, windless.

Once Again at the Stove

I'd be deadly if only I could
swing this cast iron world.
It holds old oil and sadness
and everything that
pretended to sustain us
in this logrolling.
To stop is to fall
and that's just what
I propose.
I don't mean
to hit you over
the head with it.

Make Me a Tomb of Fishes

The Germ Suspended

After René Magritte's Elective Affinities

Last night when we wed, we dived in tandem
through the O of a great oak headboard, our
nightclothes tattered and flying behind us.

Tonight I walked in on you sawing apart
the bed, several spent blades and their
broken teeth littering the floor.

That triumphant arch, now cruelly bifurcated,
shackles two of the posts, intact but severed
and affixed by some horrendous glue.

I will never understand why you made it
so pretty: two of the posts dismantled
and recombined, one as axis of pedestal,
one as cross brace. The two uprights
bracketed chessboard knights dutifully
standing guard. Where did you learn such
carpentry? Where did you store the tools?

In my one night of matrimonial rest,
and under cover of sweetness, did you

wrest from me my egg and grow it to fill
your unyielding cage, welded with no
door, no chance to hatch, feed, or ever escape.

The germ suspended, the finials are proud
that we will never sleep again. Between
the cold wires I can stroke the shell,
smooth and white as alabaster. It contains
everything. It is mine. And it will never move.

In Tidal Relief

elixir of desiccation, seawater
frays the thin layers of lips offered prostrate to a jealous sun
like jellyfish spoiled to a soup on hot jetties

peeled off indelicately, raining down
as powdered glass out of quarreling beaks
the world slips under the waves

we ignore the loss: our green pedestal darkens
and the horizon curves dizzyingly
for our floating

berating as the fence
quakes with native urchins who scatter
in the practiced nightstick wave

let the sand cram no more infant folds,
crown my flimsy land-ankles in vagrant algae
grasp my knees with tendrils

bear up my webbings and lick my hollow ears
fill my caverns and make me
a tomb of fishes

Iodine

It's a pain in the neck, what
with the goiter. Like a child
that won't be born. She dreams
of eating her clean laundry
– a form of transport. She
asks her dream companions if
it's weird. "Never my pants."
That would be too much.

Other times she's an otter who's
absentmindedly devoured her
bedding, right down to the holdfasts.
It's not the dark drift into open sea
that's frightening. It's not trusting
her ears to know if the waves
are crashing far or lapping an
imminent disaster. She's a Mary
of sorts, hands folded chest high.
If only for a stone to fondle dearly.

Iodine is the heaviest element
we can use. Accessorizing is the
hardest part. The scarves just draw

attention and she doesn't want to
seem a Grace Kelly drag parody
for piling them on. But how else
to dress while searching for halogens?

Spill

No tag and pull, nothing approaching a downward yank, just a dawning awareness of a heavy current counter to the attitude of my rod's reaching tip. A partial reel to check, and as suspected, rising in a mound, the turtle grass prop sheared or dissuaded by the brown algae, given advantage from runoff

upriver. But amidst those grey-green blades, a clown grimace of grouper. It is an unexpected catch. The biggest fish I've ever had on, and besides little rocky structure, I'm fishing from shore. The beachy slope never draws such goliaths. My trudging revolutions bring him near faster than reasonable. Is the thing

swimming toward me?

Ashore now, the fish gives way to an upright form. Tall, lithe, with flashing eyes, he speaks with apology in his strangely accustomed tenor. We are together until the turning of the tide, this new love and I.

In the morning, all the tourists are evacuated. A breach at the plant, for too long under wraps, has been proven by the loudmouth researchers to cause mutations among the sealife. The health effects to humans remain unknown.

The Smell of Honey

As nascent corpses breathe out their love
it congeals in a sticky ball with all the millions'
and goes to live in my beehive.
Cracked amphorae of thuja and clove
grow in eucalyptus mushroom rings,
chaya moths harden in violet sugar
and fall to the waiting grass,

thyme and camphor streak red
borealis, gnats in last light turn coral
spawn in moonlight, swarms spin
sleeping spiders into hing.

We inhale and never have to eat again.
When the archaeologists appraise us, they'll
know our cassia embalming by the taste
of our bark.

Florida's New Space Program

Bat centrifuge is Venus
within half parens of moon.
Canopy of too-tall palm
punches both of them
right in the bread basket.

I am swept in a sidewalk
tide of wedding-gifted wine
observing the featureless
strangers fishing for poisoned
fish in the canal. The tumbler
describes its inner slant,
point fixe in a crazy gyroscope,
call it 26.6406° N

In cobalt twilight the whole
world wants to scream:
are you touched or just simple?
If you know which, you can't
be the other – call it
Emily's divinest sense.

A neighbor spies
me, most of his belongings
on the lawn. Well, how
would I know? Except
that there's nothing
for him to make room for.
(He's gruff, I'm aloof.
But at least we have
that in common.)

Up north, I hear,
the geese have started
on their way. In some months
soon will down pad satellite of bat.

Permission to expand

if you can work on your posture you can
work on anything - stop squishing your organs

when pressure in your head oblongs your
eyes it's myopia, sounds Greek

at least it's something clinical
consider it the reverse of a telescope

a machine that makes
everything inside look big

my friend's mom hated to think about
those pulsing things working on her behalf

she died young of a heart attack but was
glad to know I had moved on from that man

even at my immediate peril. Some mechanisms
are faithful when we don't think about them

stretch your spine, make space, but you can't be
afraid of invasion. Gird nothing. Good luck.

Vengeance

I want you
prostrated
by the damp
in the yard

weeping silently
as my music
seeps out
the window
with the sweat
of my onions.

I want you
to pound
with an
impotent fist
as my glass
goes clink,
so cute
it's impossible.

I want
your tears
as verses
useless
as semen
spent
on grass.

Dry

The tropics pantomime a season, line a
nest with things fallen, found, and pinneate.
Epochs of salt excise this brittleness. How
were fronds prepared for Calusa thatch if
not through successions of distress? A downy
pelican sister trundles out its egg twin for
all the regurgitant ministrations it can get.

Someone bequeathed to us spindles of
palms, an ill-considered bauble for the
foreclosed grid of an unseen 50 years.
They shake out girded feathers that float
to easy rest in the fractured street.

Do these balanced wisps detect the burning
of their kind just inland, and panic ever up?
Smoke knits a sun dog. Such tallness is
sapsucker-pocked, and we wish to maintain
our necks so we only see their striving,

fine tinder when it falls.

Not for Long

False uprights of slatted fence,
turgid stems of green water –
membranes and buttresses desperate
tries against some distant fall.

We had set protocols of bras then
when the nurse checked for scoliosis.
Did she dream all night of ridged girls,
a braille of straight up and down,
and how did she end up here, anyway?

I think of those strobe vision drives through
Georgia, the east trees conspiring with
sunrise, the light syncing with my pulse.
Your REM twitch. The RPMs of everything.

Fast had to be the new up, the
brace of life before it got away from us,
Long never lasts. Straight, neither,
all false ballet like racks of history.

Any Migration is Forced

7 Billion

don't the gold bars go clank! in the saddle

same as the trust on a horse, when it enters water
well, it must know what it's capable of! or on the

down-cliff, angled more than one is used to, woo-hoo
echo! must know what it's doing kai oh!

sometimes it's important to remember
the country was once mapped by people

who most of all didn't want to die on the way,
makes it a miracle anyone's here at all.

Fish don't know they're one out of 30,000
TBD, not eaten by gar or man. Welcome, little one

stay as long as you can.

The Flea Market Sells our Sacred Origins from Under Us

How so many antiquities?
How - the dust, so thick,
with what mites and meteors,
a core sample of adorable brevity.

There are bells on the shop door
and it's unpardonable,
the clanging entrance,
the effect on our lungs,
pink darlings, all tender viscera.

The miner sang Clementine
and we don't sing anything
for upsetting the useless teacups
and preposterous liquidation
of human epochs.

Yet we are done in, suffocated
by the rankness of history.
What's the least you will accept?

If Blake Had Only Known

The Sundarbans tigers behave like no other tigers in the world; in fact, no other predator of any species so aggressively seeks out our kind – Sy Montgomery, Spell of the Tiger: The Man-eaters of Sundarbans

Runoff an allowance of stout geography,
amorphous as our grievances against willing new
cartographers. Everything is bound to change like

a damsel to the tracks. Once, downstream, tigers had
no taste for human flesh. The cubs now get it in the
milk. By which tributary will your bones find rest?

The migrations all follow the new water; all the
cats are related, no more need to compete. Burn
bright the mangrove torches of the honey seekers.

Too much salt in the diet has unpredictable effects.

Religion at the City Pier

Striking thing, about the baptism at the boat ramp,
how we had to wait with the skiff for the man to be
dunked under. Well, anywhere there's water.

He was walking through, feeling life wasn't going
anywhere – might as well head to the city pier, see
some brown water to slip under, unseen.

The minister was just there, doing baptisms, might
as well. The water of the river, tea from upward
oaks: tannins and muck and Jesus is everywhere.

The banks had been straightened, army corps of engineers
saving the generations from its snaking ways, spoiling
up islands in millennia of extinct horse teeth.

Some things get bigger over time, others shrink with the
evolution. Some just slip under the surface for finding.

We got our boat in, slept on the island, empty towers
lighting the distance, all foreclosed.

Night in the Tropics

Powerline horizons
mark a growing distance
from a rising moon,
slack tambourine
for a listless player.

Yellow beacons
of apartment windows
crochet a comic street
noir against a gesso
of date palms.

Dead fronds slap
barkless trunks like rakes,
shaking out the day.

A dog runs toward traffic
and unseen neighbors
all die together.
An extra second
is added to the clock.

High rises spring up
like teeth – as we
finally inhale –
false mountains
and a moon drips
off the page.

The Skill in Gravity

Vantage is a type of wood,
a sound knock of understanding,
that reverberation across
a snowy vista,
children sledding until
they meet with something solid

the ones that have seen
the other seasons,
let them set up the track

unless they've got
a score to settle.

Let the plow pile
up the snow
for a bank like a pool game
and there's the skill in gravity

that grating, the grind
under a plastic sled
until you meet the other side

the unwind
and sleep later.
Ah, winter.

Any Migration is Forced

Gravity's not downward
but a pull between. If
you're bigger than me,
I'm gonna come to you

just how it works. Don't
mind the plastic caddy of
Lysols, my multigrain will
replace your white inflammation.

Let's put some shades over
the bare hanging. I'm not
going to change you I
promise: I'll wait up.

Any migration is forced.
Diaspora is how I show
I care. Remember: I'm the
one who had to assimilate.

It's what was best. For you.

Pieces of the Poet

This is the poem you leave behind
that you die in the middle of. Would
you want to be a tea drinker, circles of
honeyed milk a slovenly notion among
the measured stacks? Expurgate by small

cauldron fire the incriminating diaries.
Plant a demure brandy flask and catalog
your correspondence with the semi-
famous author. This is your museum
of yourself. What to write? Choose one
to be your favorite pen. There's so much

your friends don't know about you. This
is the clouded window through which he
gazed at length. And this, the photo of his
long-dead wife. Cancer, young. We only
met him later. Pretty girl, though. So sad.
He had the most amazing perspective given

everything! And now, he, cut down in
his prime. He would joke about being
camouflaged on the couch. All that tweed.

Odd, the poet was a walking cliché. And
none of you ever read a word?

He had struck up a friendship with that
doctor, was working on "something
medical." What's left on his desk, then?
Just impressions on the notepad, revealed by
pencil rubbing: *succinylcholine chloride*.
Strange title. And shame he didn't get too
far with it.

7 Years for Us
For Zhu Yufu

7 years for poetry
for pumping in and out
the blood of the heart
for the exuberance
of being one among
many

the state crushes a peony
and the poet writes with that
new red ink. Subversion! to wrap
the bruise inside bolts of silk and
send it unfurling down the palace steps

see what moans there, what broken bird
within. The emperor can't have it.
Cut out blindfolds and bring your boot
down on the naked cry. The stain upon
many others cannot be discerned.

Lock down the compound. Confiscate
all flares. Stuff the mouths with sweets
and shuffle off the men to their work.
We'll show the world our synchronization.

7 years for breathing
see the number bend like a crane
for bleeding
may it swoop, then fly
for every molecule
conspiring in vibration
against the restraints
hear the wings? they push the
air past your face
7 years for Zhu Yufu
it is a white bird. An absolute
kind of white. Something of
your dreams
7 years for us.
white, as freedom

A personal Stonehenge

They accounted only for this day
when they built the house.
The other three sixty-four

they found themselves at odds:
every morning 1 missing shoe,
coffee spilled on the closet's 1 tie

on the way to work.

1 threatening neighbor
3 failed pregnancies
and zero things to say
And if on any March twenty-nine,
they failed to stand in the kitchen
across a gulf of 13 years at

exactly 7:15
they would miss the shard
of hard, equatorial sun, which,
in its transit, laid bare their
remembering.
And they often did.

This is the spot, one would say
I remember why, said the other

and four eyes, half blue,
half green, welled – "well"

and set about the task

of one more supper.

Overdone

The crack of felled things
upends my silent return.

I spent the morning
in a morose river walk
performing the usual postmortem,
putting pins into last night.

You were a felled thing, too,
and I was as ever bereaved.
But now you've got the tea on
and there's toast,
which has been overdone,
like always.

I pause, smelling the thing both
welcoming and sad,
before making the antique knob
disappear in my hand.
I can hear the shook-shook
of your attempt to undo
your mistake with a butter knife.

The curtains are too yellow,
your smile too bright,
the creak of the boards
too quaint for either of us.

And you're wearing a new apron.

Microscopic

pink proteas and ancient sturgeon
and I, so haunted, by everything antediluvian,
gills red with impossible oxygenation
the awesome disquiet of my young self
at the zoo needing a bench
(is anything that efficient anymore?)

and before even that all ferns!
what spores from any-then still
infect a soup can pyramid of red
convenience? What moss abides
through boxed corn flake rows

everything that lived still a coelacanth
until one pulls one up.

what to ask of history

when it looks you in the eye?

Sounds Like Leaving

Blue island of landing strip
the only night light acceptable
in Lutheran fields

patchworked by day
in soybeans and corn,
pious in their plaid utility.

Beveled earth is the
staid corduroy yoke of history,
waves of no water

while young men throw
down their Budweisers
to shatter in defiance of nothing
in parking lots, in pickups

chains across all the old doors.

Silos lean into a different wind
that sounds like leaving,
a motor hum growing silent
with each further hill.

Dust dances like a devil.
It always does.

Consider the Living

The jets sounded pilotless this morning
as we buried one of the breeding stock.

We'd like to rise up like privateers against
the scurrilous machinations of the airport
ferrying its privilege. But we're not at war
with the world. We have papers.

This city lot contains all our authority,
we've seen it through from seed to deed.
The chickens scratch over the mound for
fresh worms. The bank won't come today,

we got a continuance.

Blizzard, 2015

Cicadas I hear all the time.
Up north the heat bees singed the pine
when the trails became difficult with rain

Florida is ringed with tinnitus,
the insects claiming all seasons,
and the ads for hearing aids and tweed couches,
doilies yellowed with ill advised relatives

Those mountains were kept frost-heaved in mud
and silence, the ladder rungs of latitudes littered
with gill nets, vasectomies and turtles
crossing for new water

The roads north closed by snow,
the airports don't know where to put it.

Bury Me in the Sky

Hold tight to the dream
with the balled fists
of an infant. Prayer flags tatter
as bald griffons in search
of those things earth
loves to offer sky – life
that fed now feeds
and is carried as mudra.

Bring me those bones.

May you stoop to enter
a hundred mud-framed
doors greeted by the deep
wrinkles of a smiling Tibet,
the generous fat of a mother
yak melting into ever more
generous tea. If a lama is

laughing, it is in a far place
and China is just a tag
inside your dress and no one's
yet said "Namaste."

These peaks are mudra, earth,
all fault, sutures and boundary
thrust, growing bones
from the feet on up forever
giving birth to itself
on the roof of the world.

I was born a new infant
on the roof of your Empire
State, wine glass a disabused
vessel, spirit transmigrated,
your fists balled up, wrinkles
deepening, coloring like mud.

There's no disinterring what
can never be buried. No soil.
Exposure the only work of time.
The dream does not climb,

can only be scuttled. If
this ship lands on any rocks,
it will be at 12,000 feet
where no water bubbles up.

Dedication

For dead dogs
and stolen children,
a special heaven
with rubber balls
and each other.

Sargasso

Pristine Creature

Here we are pummeled
by the left hand of the weather –
all power, no control.

The edge of the bridge
carries up the rain,
a slate tombstone to the sky.

We stand like suicides reconsidering
as traffic soaks us more
speeding to a various destiny.

Once was I a pristine creature,
haloed in gold leaf beyond a velvet rope.
But, the ennui of pricelessness!

Defame me, deframe me,
cut me away from the signatured canvas,
away from this marriage of cultish objects.

Let my cup spill and clang on the marble,
send the watchman running.
Hang me crooked above a motel bed.

Does my gilding gleam too
in the glow of neon signage?
The color of commerce – red,
it feels sexy.

What have I sacrificed
for the tousled sheets:
your eyes from an engraved bench.
But you have lost everything

when your muse won't stay
in the museum.

Hepatic Portal Dreaming

Do peristalsis with some originality,
contract like a boa from the inguinal
attachments. Interstitial quilting is
by some fancy needle!

Remember the teacher who
said you could drink from a cup,
standing on your head? Don't try
this at home but such knowledge.

Swallowing works even up,
plantar surfaces upwards.
Everything needs a decent
airing out. Never on Sunday

and daylight will never come
but always does too soon.
Negotiate a nap, you little sneak.
But the pulsing is transplanted,

permanent. No chance of rejection.

Sargasso

My heart is shadows of clouds,
thin vapors hiding the sun.
My heart is horizon,
a peeling back of the skin of day,
and the beach for a soft landing.

It is the duress of slaves on a ship
or it is the oars and the whip.

Am I compelled to or from you?

You are neither destination nor origin
but Sargasso, a swirling eye of ocean,
that confounds the efforts
of all my sweating, displaced natives,
huge men they are, my heart,
plucked from an ignorant Eden.

You are all Coriolis and seaweed.
I am all faulty navigation:
earnest haste thickly mired.

My heart is hummingbirds all slowed down.

Husk of a Whale

I loved you like a war zone is haunted,
full of the unknowing dead. A leviathan
isn't supposed to die: get big as a 16-wheeler
and you set an example. Rivers traverse

counties inlaid by slavery and ill-financed
railroads; the tracks still birth flowers
of bees. Washing up it revealed over seven
days the secrets of a stinking God –

as big as we think we are, oxygen is common
currency. I stood atop Florida's ridge
like a desert skink, looked upon
a tower from every angle of the working

class. In the rain the ground would not
stop rising, the tower now used for cell
phones, its bells consigned to rust, the bones
of its shadows mined like phosphate grants
purchase on shifting sand. The peninsula

slips its skin, beaches a husk of whale. Once,
the fossils tell us, there were mammoths.

Texas Radio, 1971
With a little help from Jim Morrison

Out here shadows escape their makers
and scale into snakes. You can see them
only in the perimeter, fleeting. No one
can let loose their focus for more
than half a second. I'll tell you this:

we are hard-wired for wasting the dawn.
Our shadows do not attempt escape,
for we are not the trees, whose shadow-snakes
eat stars before morning and rabbits
all night, before again holding down
the shaky roots of trees. Out here
in the perimeter there are no
rabbits. Out here snakes eat stones
immaculate. Now listen to this:

anarchy is a rusted bus full of flowers.
Silence, silk, spider-spun. Cactus stabs
the air forever. Tumbleweed somersaults
in search of shadow, wandering, wandering
in hopeless night. You and I know: it's coiled
under a ledge perennially full of strike,
sudden fury of divine messenger.

I'll tell you about Texas radio and the big beat,
the last big beat and the slow bathtub ripple
in a Paris apartment that tells us this: out here
we IS hard-wired for shadow.

Dark Island Landing

In forest edge dark
The god screeches.
the frogs,
the night lilies,
the open throated
children to the suckling sky

are my dreams of
being broken
of being backwards
on a boat
over the wake,

the huff of an
incessant horse
that smells like
earnestness

and it is fear
or trust
that is his food.

He grazes indifferently
for he forgets
the taste of grass.

All There Is

mistake intention for actual memory

the lack of speed is frightening,
running to deal with the crisis,
not getting there fast enough

and you never did turn on the tea.

There are monks who say if you
didn't get enough early on in life,
you need anchoring to the earth.

You need buttered broths and to
copy old writings by hand by
very poor light.

Ruin your eyes

it always comes back to the mother

somehow.

We're not equipped to

deal with speeding trains, that step
off the platform always the skirting
of two unknowns

one of going, one of coming away
and no – it's not the same thing.

The relief of meeting with something
solid. Let them step over my fetal
form. All the subway police need to know:

here is all there is.

Acknowledgments

Thank you to the editors of the following magazines, in which some of these poems have appeared, sometimes in different forms:

A-Minor Magazine, Bending Genres Journal, Blue Fifth Review, cur-ren-cy, Dead Snakes, DOGZPLOT, Do Hookers Kiss?, Drunk Monkeys, Foxglove Journal, Leveler, Mad Hatters Review, Mad Rush, Metazen, MockingHeart Review, Mojave River Review, Museum Life, Nixes Mate Review, Pipe Dreams Publishing, Psychic Meatloaf, Ramshackle Review, Right Hand Pointing, Short, Fast, and Deadly; The Anenome Sidecar, The Bamboo Forest, The Camel Saloon, The Smoking Poet, THIS Literary Magazine, Wilderness House Literary Review.

I owe a debt of gratitude to my friends and family, especially my mom for insisting I keep on with my early fits and starts, Dr. Marlowe Miller for insisting that I'm "hot shit," John for insisting I get on a plane and go be with my writer family, the All City Crew for insisting I write every damn week, and my son Rhys for being my North Star.

Joani Reese once lovingly demanded, "Bring me those bones," leading to the namesake poem of this collection.

Meg Tuite, Len Kuntz, Robert Vaughan, Karen Stefano, Jen Knox, Martha Jackson Kaplan, John Van Wagner, Oliver Knudsen – you all are just so good. I am fortunate to have many more mentors than I could ever name here. But as long as we're "Listing," I need to send my love to John Davis. Thanks ever for your encouragement.

Thank you to Nixes Mate Books for all the beauty.

About the Author

Originally from Massachusetts, Sara Comito lives in Fort Myers, Florida, where she and her husband have a small urban farm and work together in their natural stone masonry business. This is her first collection.

42° 19' 47.9" N   70° 56' 43.9" W

Nixes Mate is a navigational hazard in Boston Harbor used during the colonial period to gibbet and hang pirates and mutineers.

Nixes Mate Books features small-batch artisanal literature, created by writers who use all 26 letters of the alphabet and then some, honing their craft the time-honored way: one line at a time.

nixesmate.pub/books

www.ingramcontent.com/pod-product-compliance
Lightning Source LLC
Chambersburg PA
CBHW050332120526
44592CB00014B/2156